IRAN WILL BE FREE

SPEECH BY

MARYAM RAJAVI

PARIS, FRANCE
JUNE 30, 2018

Iran Will Be Free: Speech by Maryam Rajavi

Copyright © National Council of Resistance of Iran – U.S. Representative Office, 2018.

All rights reserved. No part of this monograph may be used or reproduced in any manner whatsoever without written permission except in the case of brief quotations embodied in articles or reviews.

First published in 2018 by
National Council of Resistance of Iran - U.S. Representative Office (NCRI-US), 1747 Pennsylvania Ave., NW, Suite 1125, Washington, DC 20006

ISBN-10 (hard cover): 1-944942-21-1
ISBN-13 (hard cover): 978-1-944942-21-2

ISBN-10 (paperback): 1-944942-20-3
ISBN-13 (paperback): 978-1-944942-20-5

ISBN-10 (eBook): 1-944942-22-X
ISBN-13 (eBook): 978-1-944942-22-9

Library of Congress Control Number: 2018956911

Library of Congress Cataloging-in-Publication Data

National Council of Resistance of Iran - U.S. Representative Office.
The Regime's Overthrow Is Certain, Iran Will Be Free: Speech by Maryam Rajavi

1. Iran. 2. Democracy. 3. Human rights. 4. Women rights. 5. Religion

First Edition: September 2018

Printed in the United States of America

These materials are being distributed by the National Council of Resistance of Iran-U.S. Representative Office. Additional information is on file with the Department of Justice, Washington, D.C.

Table of Contents

5	**1. Introduction**
9	**2. Maryam Rajavi's Speech**
10	2.1. Greetings
12	2.2. The leverage for overthrow
14	2.3. The persistence of the uprising
16	2.4. An explosive and irreversible situation
18	2.5. The collapse of the appeasement policy
19	2.6. The fuel to the fire of the uprisings
22	2.7. The overthrow requires resistance units
26	2.8. National Solidarity Front
29	2.9. The people's violated sovereignty must be revived
31	2.10. Place everything at the service of the uprisings
35	**3. Ten-Point Plan for the Future of Iran**
39	**4. A Brief Bio of Maryam Rajavi**
43	**5. About the NCRI-US**
45	**6. List of Publications of NCRI-US**

Introduction

1

INTRODUCTION

On Saturday, June 30, 2018, the Iranian Resistance's grand gathering was held in Villepinte, near Paris, France. Delegations from various countries including prominent politicians, members of parliaments, mayors, elected representatives, and international experts on Iran and the Middle East attended the event.

The speakers declared their support for the Iranian people's uprising and the democratic alternative, the National Council of Resistance of Iran.

Mrs. Maryam Rajavi, the president-elect of the National Council of Resistance of Iran, delivered the keynote speech. This manuscript contains the full text of Mrs. Rajavi's remarks.

Maryam Rajavi's Speech

2

2.1. Greetings

My fellow compatriots,
Dear friends,
Elected representatives, honorable dignitaries from around the world,

Greetings to all of you and to my dear compatriots in Iran and all over the world. The first thing that must be said today is that the flames of the auspicious and liberating uprising are again rising in Tehran and across Iran: Once again in Mashhad and Shiraz, Bandar Abbas and Qeshm, Karaj and Kermanshah, Shahriar, Islamshahr, Kashan, Arak, Isfahan, Ram Hormuz, and many other towns and cities.

Indeed, the flames of the protests cannot be extinguished and they will continue to soar without respite, indicating a constantly expanding and deepening uprising.

The thunderous voices of rebellious youths in various cities represent the beating heart of a nation immersed in the euphoria of a free Iran.

Once again, I salute my fellow compatriots in Khorramshahr, who are thirsting for clean drinking water and for freedom. You unequivocally told the mullahs that their prayers are not acceptable in the eyes of God.

I have come here on behalf of a Resistance movement which has offered its entire existence to secure victory for the Iran uprising, and for Iran's freedom, pride, and magnificence.

I have come here to reiterate what you seek: The time has come for the regime's overthrow. Victory is certain and Iran will be free.

We salute the People's Mojahedin Organization of Iran (PMOI/MEK) members in Ashraf 3, the home of the passionate (in Albania). Congratulations for constructing it with your own hands.

Onwards with the 1,000 Ashrafs (resistance units) in our occupied homeland.

2.2. The leverage for overthrow

Since the January uprising, the peak of the volcano of change and the regime's overthrow in Iran has emerged. The triumph of Iran's democratic revolution, without sheikhs or shahs, is now looming on the horizon. Through their uprisings and relying on resistance units, the Iranian people are employing the leverage they need to topple this regime.

How and where can we discover these realities?

First, owing to the presence of the Resistance movement, the charade billed as the existence of a "solution" within the religious fascism has been debunked.

> First, owing to the presence of the Resistance movement, the charade billed as the existence of a "solution" within the religious fascism has been debunked.

The rebellious population and youth have rejected both factions of the regime. These are the same fearless youth who have chosen the path of fighting on, going on the maximum offensive, and waging resistance regardless of the cost.

2.3. The persistence of the uprising and the protest movement despite maximum suppression

The second sign that the era of the regime's overthrow has arrived is that for the past six months the Iranian people have waged an uprising and a protest movement despite the imposition of maximum suppression, despite the so-called "suicides" of the detainees in the mullahs' prisons and despite daily arrests and executions designed to intimidate the public.

The workers at Haft-Tapeh sugar cane factory resumed their uprising. Then, the workers at Ahvaz steel factory, and farmers in Isfahan rose up. Worshipers in Isfahan turned their backs on Khamenei's Friday prayer leader and chanted: "My back to the enemy and face to the nation."

Isfahan Province was still on edge when our Arab compatriots in Khuzestan, especially in Ahvaz, rose up. Then came Kurdistan as the lengthy strike in Baneh aroused everyone's admiration. Then, on the roadmap to overthrow, a new role

> The second sign that the era of the regime's overthrow has arrived is that for the past six months the Iranian people have waged an uprising and a protest movement despite the imposition of maximum suppression...

model emerged: Kazerun, the city of uprising, fire and blood, with audacious women, who alongside their brothers and rocks in hand, repelled the heavily-armed enemy forces, imitating the resistance we saw at Camp Ashraf.

At that moment, the uprising accelerated. The strike by toiling truck drivers and owners in 285 cities and in 31 provinces shook the regime to its foundation for 12 days.

Teachers, retirees, defrauded investors, and workers of hundreds of manufacturing units rose up day after day. And last week, the Tehran bazaar rose up and ignited an uprising in Tehran and other cities.

Iran revolted once again, with all its children, with all its nationalities and ethnicities.

Truly, what is the destination? The answer is: A free Iran, through the eradication of all the facets of dictatorship and plundering policies, and by bringing down Khamenei from power.

2.4. An explosive and irreversible situation

The third sign of the inevitable overthrow of the ruling religious fascism is that social tensions and economic crises, especially high prices, unemployment, poverty, and inequality have reached a critical mass.

Everyone senses the explosive state of society. And the mullahs can offer neither a solution nor are willing or able to resolve the problems.

The **velayat-e faqih** (absolute clerical rule) lacks all legitimacy. Khamenei's standing has plummeted dramatically. The regime has

> The third sign of the inevitable overthrow of the ruling religious fascism is that social tensions and economic crises, especially high prices, unemployment, poverty, and inequality have reached a critical mass.

run out of cash. The Revolutionary Guards and the unpopular Bassij forces have been facing defections. The masquerade of "moderation" designed to preserve the regime has now been unmasked. And the regime in its entirety is drowning in the abyss of internal feuds and bickering.

And now, it is the regime's own advocates who are confessing that there are two rival governments at the apex of the ruling establishment. One regime advocate openly said: "We are getting close to a watershed moment that will see the ouster of one of the two governments, and either the hidden government will take full control of administering the affairs, or it will be forced to relinquish portions of its authority."

2.5. The collapse of the appeasement policy

The fourth sign of the phase of the regime's overthrow is that internationally, the mullahs have lost the most important backer of the policy of appeasement, namely the United States.

The international shield safeguarding the regime has fallen by the way side. The mullahs have practically lost their JCPOA. The avalanche of successive sanctions is hitting them hard, undercutting their ability to engage in warmongering and adventurism in the region. An arms and oil embargo, demanded by the Iranian Resistance for four decades, is now in the process of being somewhat implemented. And the era of labeling, bombing and suppressing the opposition at the behest of the regime and for the benefit of the regime has come to an end.

> The fourth sign of the phase of the regime's overthrow is that internationally, the mullahs have lost the most important backer of the policy of appeasement, namely the United States.

2.6. The Blood of the martyrs and suffering of those detained fuel the fire of the uprisings

The fifth and most important indication that the mullahs' regime has entered the era of overthrow is that the very development the mullahs have feared the most is now a reality; that is, the link and relationship between the fury of the deprived and oppressed on the one hand and the organized Resistance movement on the other. All regime leaders and junior and senior officials have repeatedly acknowledged to this fact. This is their way of admitting that the regime's rule is nearing its end.

Indeed, the regime is on the brink of overthrow.

Prior to this, in 2013, following the massacre of 52 PMOI members at Camp Ashraf, when several residents were taken hostage, Massoud Rajavi announced the roadmap for creating 1,000 Ashrafs (resistance units) inside Iran so that the organization that leads the uprising could be linked to the arisen people of Iran. Accordingly, units and councils for the national resistance became the tip of the spear of

> **The fifth and most important indication that the mullahs' regime has entered the era of overthrow is that ...**
>
> **... the link and relationship between the fury of the deprived and oppressed on the one hand and the organized Resistance movement on the other.**

the strategy for uprising and overthrow in the cities which have risen up in revolt in Iran. This is how the blood of the martyrs and the suffering of those detained since June 20, 1981 until today, are fueling the uprisings. As Massoud Rajavi said, "If Iran stands, the world will stand with us and by our side."

A euphoric generation thirsting for freedom has risen up. Those taking part in the uprising joined by resistance units have now charted a new territory. Rise up and walk along this path. Join hands with them and heed their call for a free Iran; declare your readiness.

You saw when the people of Varzaneh took over the city's entry points. Kazerunis took over the streets, and truck drivers and owners took over the highways. And you saw how the young people in Tehran, in Lalehzar, Ferdowsi, Shoush, Mellat and Ekbatan exhibited enormous courage in confronting the ruthless security agents, building barricades in the streets.

This is the Iranian nation's fight to capture the entire country and take back Iran from the occupiers, the mullahs.

2.7. The overthrow of this regime requires resistance units and a liberation army

These days, an industry concocting phony alternatives has become prevalent in the political arena, of course copying and pasting aspects from others. And this in itself is another sign of the phase of the regime's overthrow. But the crux of the matter is how they are going to actually bring down this regime in practice. This question is especially relevant as the blood of the martyrs has permanently and historically blocked the path to reform within the clerical regime and the return of the monarchy.

Now, if one can topple this regime without an organization and leadership, without overcoming thorny trials, and without paying the price and making sacrifices, we say: Please, go ahead, don't delay.

If one can restore the people's sovereignty without a history of fighting against two regimes, without drawing boundaries against dictatorship, subordination and dependency; without waging a nationwide resistance and offering a galaxy of martyrs, without challenging the principle of the velayat-e faqih and phony regime "moderates," we say: Please, go ahead, don't delay.

> **Now, if one can topple this regime without an organization and leadership, without overcoming thorny trials, and without paying the price and making sacrifices, we say: Please, go ahead, don't delay.**

If one can topple the mullahs without challenging Khomeini over the unpatriotic Iran-Iraq war, forcing an end to the inferno of that war; and discrediting the regime's slogan of "liberating Qods via Karbala"; without compelling Khomeini to accept the ceasefire by launching 100 military operations by the National Liberation Army of Iran, which captured the city of Mehran and marched to the gates of Kermanshah; and without exposing the regime's nuclear weapons, missile, chemical and microbiological programs and facilities: Yes, go ahead and don't delay.

If one can leapfrog a fifty-year history overnight and create real change in Iran while dreaming about foreign support, and without having to expose the regime's human rights abuses and crimes in 64 UN resolutions, without the campaign for justice for the massacre of political prisoners in 1988, without campaigns by supporters of the resistance worldwide and insisting on the rights of the Iranian nation for four decades, without the specific platform and programs of the NCRI and the Provisional Government for the transition of sovereignty to the Iranian people, and finally without a tested leader, who has guided this ferocious struggle for five decades, if all of this can instead be done overnight, we say: Go ahead, the ball is in your court.

But let me say this: Such a fantasy is only possible through an Iraq-like occupation, or in other words through a foreign intervention. The aftermath of that scenario is already known.

Over the past 40 years, all those aspiring opponents who were nonetheless unwilling to pay the price have had opportunities to test their luck. But the hard realities and real experiences have shown that this dark and evil regime will neither be reformed nor turn "green" or "velvet."

The overthrow of this regime inevitably requires a willingness to pay the necessary price, it requires the practice of honesty and sacrifice, it requires an organization and a sturdy political alternative, and it requires the organization of resistance units and an army of liberation.

> The overthrow of this regime inevitably requires a willingness to pay the necessary price...

Nevertheless, as Massoud Rajavi said in the context of evaluating the January uprising:

"We are not in competition with anyone seeking to assume power. On the other hand and most certainly, no one can compete with the PMOI when it comes to practicing honesty, sacrifice and paying the price."

> "We are not in competition with anyone seeking to assume power. On the other hand and most certainly, no one can compete with the PMOI when it comes to practicing honesty, sacrifice and paying the price."
>
> — Massoud Rajavi

2.8. National Solidarity Front to overthrow the religious dictatorship

Sixteen years ago, the Iranian Resistance adopted a plan called the National Solidarity Front for the Overthrow of the Ruling Religious Dictatorship and declared that it was prepared to cooperate with all forces who want a republic, who are committed to the complete rejection of the velayat-e faqih regime and who struggle for a democratic, independent Iran, based on separation of religion and state.

Over the past four decades, the NCRI, beyond typical political rhetoric, has paid a heavy price in blood and treasure for each and every one of its declarations, ratifications and commitments.

We call for the establishment of a society based on freedom, democracy, and equality, which has clear demarcation lines against despotism and dependence as well as gender, ethnic and class discrimination. We have defended and will continue to defend gender equality, the right to freely choose one's attire, separation of religion and state, autonomy of nationalities, equal political and social rights for all citizens of Iran, abolition of the death penalty, freedom of expression, parties, the media, assembly, unions, associations, councils and syndicates.

The NCRI's 12-point plan for the autonomy of Iranian Kurdistan, adopted and announced 35 years ago, remains one of the most comprehensive examples globally for addressing the rights of nationalities. And, in the end, a free and non-nuclear Iran will promote peaceful coexistence with its neighbors, and would embrace regional and international cooperation.

This is the image of the democratic alternative, which rejects the mullahs' rule or any form of dictatorship.

On this path, the first step is to transfer sovereignty to the people of Iran. By relying on the Iranian people and a popular social base, one can avert chaos and insecurity and safeguard the integrity of Iran and Iranians, rendering it a proud nation.

According to the NCRI's program, following the regime's overthrow, a provisional six-month government will be formed, whose primary task is to form a constituent assembly through free elections on the basis of a popular, direct, equal and secret

> ... following the regime's overthrow, a provisional six-month government will be formed, whose primary task is to form a constituent assembly through free elections ...

ballot. This constituent assembly must draft the constitution of the new republic within two years and put it to a popular vote. It must also set up the principal institutions of the new republic based on the people's vote.

2.9. The people's violated sovereignty of the Iranian people must be revived

We believe it is possible to eradicate high prices, poverty, unemployment, shanty towns, water shortages and environmental calamities. But, before anything else, the trampled political rights, specifically the right to sovereignty of the Iranian people, must be restored and revived. This is the aim of our Resistance and the raison d'etre for the NCRI.

But the Iranian regime has benefitted the most by denying the wherewithal of this Resistance and this alternative and by using western appeasers to suppress this movement.

> ... the task of overthrowing the regime, bringing about democratic change and establishing a free Iran rests on our own shoulders and those of the Iranian people.

Therefore, as far as Iran in concerned, without recognizing the Resistance and the right to resist, the damages that the policy of appeasement has so far inflicted on the Iranian people cannot be rectified.

As we have always stated, and I reiterate here, the task of overthrowing the regime, bringing about democratic change and establishing a free Iran rests on our own shoulders and those of the Iranian people.

At the same time, we would welcome any retreat by the mullahs because one thousand chalices of poison would ultimately serve the interests of 1,000 Ashrafs (resistance units).

Today, the brave youth of Iran have completely dedicated themselves to the task of sustaining the uprising.

I hail the courageous women of Iran, who are leading the way everywhere. I also hail the young people and members of resistance units, who even while in captivity insist on declaring their PMOI identity, which terrifies the regime.

> Today, the brave youth of Iran have completely dedicated themselves to the task of sustaining the uprising.

2.10. Place everything at the service of the uprisings, giving it all we have, to advance the uprising

I call upon all of you to provide practical support to the uprisings. All Iranians, wherever they are, can help and advance the uprising. Also, you, the Iranian youth, who are present here, can do a lot. This is our collective commitment and our collective pledge to the Iranian nation to place everything at the service of the uprisings, giving it all we have and making sacrifices in all fronts in order to advance the uprising.

Literally, every single one of us will be with the uprising every moment and every second of every day.

I hail all the martyrs and defiant prisoners from June 20, 1981, until today. I hail those eternal flames of love, Sediqeh Mojaveri and Neda Hassani, on the 15th anniversary of their martyrdom. May their memories and names last forever!

I am well aware that your unsparing emotions are directed at the galaxy of martyrs of the Resistance and the Iranian people's liberation army as well as those in the uprisings, the resistance units and the steadfast and persevering prisoners, especially those massacred in 1988 in the regime's prisons 30 years ago.

From the depths of the dark night
A rose blossoms
Winter will no doubt pass, and
The harbinger of spring, thousands of roses in hand, will certainly follow

Hail to freedom
Hail to the people of Iran
Hail to all of you.

Ten-Point Plan for the Future of Iran

1 In our view, the ballot box is the only criterion for legitimacy. Accordingly, we seek a republic based on universal suffrage.

2 We want a pluralist system, freedom of parties and assembly. We respect all individual freedoms. We underscore complete freedom of expression and of the media and unconditional access by all to the internet.

3 We support and are committed to abolition of the death penalty.

4 We are committed to the separation of Religion and State. Any form of discrimination against the followers of any religion or denomination will be prohibited.

5 We believe in complete gender equality in political, social and economic arenas. We are also committed to equal participation of women in political leadership. Any form of discrimination against women will be abolished. They will enjoy the right to freely choose their clothing. They are free in marriage, divorce, education and employment.

6 We believe in the rule of law and justice. We want to set up a modern judicial system based on the principles of presumption of innocence, the right to defense, effective judicial protection and the right to be tried in a public court. We also seek the total independence of judges. The mullahs' Sharia law will be abolished.

7 We are committed to the Universal Declaration of Human Rights, and international covenants and conventions, including the International Covenant on Civil and Political Rights, the Convention against Torture, and the Convention on the Elimination of all Forms of Discrimination against Women. We are committed to the equality of all ethnicities. We underscore the plan for the autonomy of Iranian Kurdistan, adopted by the National Council of Resistance of Iran. The language and culture of our compatriots from whatever ethnicity are among our nation's human resources and must be revived and enhanced in tomorrow's Iran.

8 We recognize private property, private investment and the market economy. All Iranian people must enjoy equal opportunity in employment and in business ventures. We will protect and revitalize the environment.

9 Our foreign policy will be based on peaceful coexistence, international and regional peace and cooperation, as well as respect for the United Nations Charter.

10 We want a non-nuclear Iran, free of weapons of mass destruction.

Maryam Rajavi is the President-elect of the National Council of Resistance of Iran (NCRI), a coalition of some 500 Iranian opposition groups and personalities, committed to a democratic, secular and non-nuclear republic in Iran. Half of NCRI's members are women. The Council's primary task is to hold free and fair elections for a Legislative and National Constituent Assembly in Iran no more than six months after the ouster of the ruling theocracy.

A Brief Bio of Maryam Rajavi

4

Mrs. Maryam Rajavi is the President-elect of the National Council of Resistance of Iran, which seeks the establishment of a democratic, secular and non-nuclear republic in Iran.

As a Muslim woman, she advocates tolerance, gender equality and separation of religion and state.

Mrs. Rajavi was politically active during and after the 1979 revolution. She received a Bachelor's degree in Metallurgical Engineering from Sharif University of Technology in Tehran.

She was a candidate during the first parliamentary elections after the revolution and received approximately a quarter million votes, despite widespread election fraud by the Iranian regime.

Based in Paris, France, Mrs. Rajavi has appeared before many national parliaments in Europe, including the United Kingdom, Germany, Italy, Spain, Belgium, Switzerland, the Netherlands, Norway, Finland, and Canada. She has also been a frequent guest speaker at the European Parliament and the Parliamentary Assembly of the Council of Europe as well as France's National Assembly and the Senate. Mrs. Rajavi testified via satellite link before the U.S. House of Representatives Subcommittee on Terrorism, Non-proliferation and Trade.

Mrs. Rajavi lost two of her sisters in the struggle to bring freedom and democracy to Iran. One, pregnant at the time, was executed by the Ayatollahs' regime. Another was executed by the Shah's regime. A sister-in-law was executed in Iran during the 1988 massacre of political prisoners, and a brother-in-law was assassinated in 1990 by the Iranian regime's terrorists in Geneva, Switzerland.

Mrs. Rajavi has published several books, many of which are translated to multiple languages.

About the NCRI-US

5

The National Council of Resistance of Iran-US Representative Office acts as the Washington office for Iran's parliament-in-exile, which is dedicated to the establishment of a democratic, secular, non-nuclear republic in Iran.

NCRI-US, registered as a non-profit tax-exempt organization, has been instrumental in exposing the nuclear weapons program of Iran, including the sites in Natanz, and Arak, the biological and chemical weapons program of Iran, as well as its ambitious ballistic missile program.

NCRI-US has also exposed the terrorist network of the Iranian regime, including its involvement in the bombing of Khobar Towers in Saudi Arabia, the Jewish Community Center in Argentina, its fueling of sectarian violence in Iraq and Syria, and its malign activities in other parts of the Middle East.

Our office has provided information on the human rights violations in Iran, extensive anti-government demonstrations, and the movement for democratic change in Iran.

Visit our website at www.ncrius.org

You may follow us on   twitter   @ncrius

Follow us on   facebook   NCRIUS

You can also find us on   Instagram NCRIUS

List of Publications of NCRI-US

6

List of Publications by the National Council of Resistance of Iran, U.S. Representative Office

Iran's Ballistic Buildup: The March Toward Nuclear-Capable Missiles

May 2018, 136 pages

This unique manuscript surveys Iran's missile capabilities, including the underlying organization, structure, production, development infrastructure, launch facilities and command centers. The book exposes the nexus between the regime's missile activities and its nuclear weapons program, including Tehran's ties with Pyongyang.

Iran: Cyber Repression: How the IRGC Uses Cyberwarfare to Preserve the Theocracy

February 2018, 70 pages

This manuscript demonstrates how the Iranian regime, under the supervision and guidance of the IRGC and the Ministry of Intelligence and Security (MOIS), have employed new cyberwarfare and tactics in a desperate attempt to counter the growing dissent inside the country.

LIST OF PUBLICATIONS OF NCRI-US

Iran: Where Mass Murderers Rule:
The 1988 Massacre of 30,000 Political Prisoners and the Continuing Atrocities

November 2017, 161 pages

Iran: Where Mass Murderers Rule is an expose of the current rulers of Iran and their track record in human rights violations. The book details how 30,000 political prisoners fell victim to politicide during the summer of 1988 and showcases the egregious political extinction of a group of people.

Iran's Nuclear Core: Uninspected Military Sites, Vital to the Nuclear Weapons Program

October 2017, 52 pages

This book details how the nuclear weapons program is at the heart of, and not parallel to, the civil nuclear program of Iran. The program has been run by the Islamic Revolutionary Guards Corp (IRGC) since the beginning, and the main nuclear sites and nuclear research facilities have been hidden from the eyes of the United Nations nuclear watchdog.

Terrorist Training Camps in Iran: How Islamic Revolutionary Guards Corps Trains Foreign Fighters to Export Terrorism

June 1017, 56 pages

The book details how Islamic Revolutionary Guards Corps trains foreign fighters in 15 various camps in Iran to export terrorism. The IRGC has created a large directorate within its extraterritorial arm, the Quds Force, in order to expand its training of foreign mercenaries as part of the strategy to step up its meddling abroad in Syria, Iraq, Yemen, Bahrain, Afghanistan and elsewhere.

Presidential Elections in Iran: Changing Faces; Status Quo Policies
May 2017, 78 pages

The book reviews the past 11 presidential elections, demonstrating that the only criterion for qualifying as a candidate is practical and heartfelt allegiance to the Supreme Leader. An unelected vetting watchdog, the Guardian Council makes that determination.

The Rise of Iran's Revolutionary Guards' Financial Empire: How the Supreme Leader and the IRGC Rob the People to Fund International Terror
March 2017, 174 pages

This manuscript examines some vital factors and trends, including the overwhelming and accelerating influence (especially since 2005) of the Supreme Leader and the Islamic Revolutionary Guard Corps (IRGC). This study shows how ownership of property in various spheres of the economy is gradually shifted from the population writ large towards a minority ruling elite comprised of the Supreme Leader's office and the IRGC, using 14 powerhouses, and how the money ends up funding terrorism worldwide.

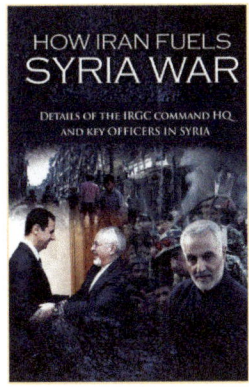

How Iran Fuels Syria War: Details of the IRGC Command HQ and Key Officers in Syria
November 2016, 74 pages

This book examines how the Iranian regime has effectively engaged in the military occupation of Syria by marshaling 70,000 forces, including the Islamic Revolutionary Guard Corps (IRGC) and mercenaries from other countries into Syria; is paying monthly salaries to over 250,000 militias and agents to prolong the conflict; and divided the country into 5 zones of conflict, establishing 18 command, logistics and operations centers.

Nowruz 2016 with the Iranian Resistance: Hoping for a New Day, Freedom and Democracy in Iran
April 2016, 36 pages

This book describes Iranian New Year, Nowruz celebrations at the Washington office of Iran's parliament-in-exile, the National Council of Resistance of Iran. The yearly event marks the beginning of spring. It includes select speeches by dignitaries who have attended the NCRIUS Nowruz celebrations. This book also discusses the very rich culture and the traditions associated with Nowruz for centuries.

The 2016 Vote in Iran's Theocracy: An analysis of Parliamentary & Assembly of Experts Elections

February 2016, 70 pages

This book examines all the relevant data about the 2016 Assembly of Experts as well as Parliamentary elections ahead of the February 2016 elections. It looks at the history of elections since the revolution in 1979 and highlights the current intensified infighting among the various factions of the Iranian regime.

IRAN: A Writ of Deception and Cover-up: Iranian Regime's Secret Committee Hid Military Dimensions of its Nuclear Program

February 2016, 30 pages

The book provides details about a top-secret committee in charge of forging the answers to the International Atomic Energy Agency (IAEA) regarding the Possible Military Dimensions (PMD) of Tehran's nuclear program, including those related to the explosive detonators called EBW (Exploding Bridge Wire) detonator, which is an integral part of a program to develop an implosion type nuclear device.

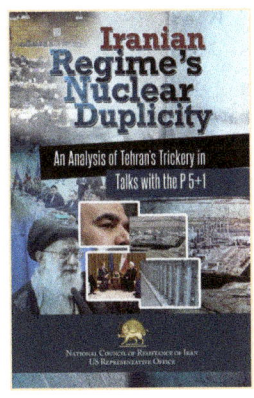

Iranian Regime's Nuclear Duplicity: An Analysis of Tehran's Trickery in Talks with the P 5+1

January 2016, 74 pages

This book examines Iran's behavior throughout the negotiations process in an effort to inform the current dialogue on a potential agreement. Drawing on both publicly available sources and those within Iran, the book focuses on two major periods of intense negotiations with the regime: 2003-2004 and 2013-2015. Based on this evidence, it then extracts the principles and motivations behind Tehran's approach to negotiations as well as the tactics used to trick its counterparts and reach its objectives.

Key to Countering Islamic Fundamentalism: Maryam Rajavi? Testimony To The U.S. House Foreign Affairs Committee

June 2015, 68 pages

Testimony before U.S. House Foreign Affairs Committee's subcommittee on Terrorism, non-Proliferation, and Trade discussing ISIS and Islamic fundamentalism. The book contains Maryam Rajavi's full testimony as well as the question and answer by representatives.

Meet the National Council of Resistance of Iran

June 2014, 150 pages

Meet the National Council of Resistance of Iran discusses what NCRI stands for, what its platform is, and why a vision for a free, democratic, secular, non-nuclear republic in Iran would serve world peace.

How Iran Regime Cheated the World: Tehran's Systematic Efforts to Cover Up its Nuclear Weapons Program

June 2014, 50 pages

This book deals with one of the most fundamental challenges that goes to the heart of the dispute regarding the Iranian regime's controversial nuclear program: to ascertain with certainty that Tehran will not pursue a nuclear bomb. Such an assurance can only be obtained through specific steps taken by Tehran in response to the international community's concerns. The monograph discusses the Iranian regime's report card as far as it relates to being transparent when addressing the international community's concerns about the true nature and the ultimate purpose of its nuclear program